洞月亮

CAVE MOON PRESS

YAKIMA 中 WASHINGTON

2017

Praise for *Habitat Lost*

Carol Alexander's collection *Habitat Lost* gives us memorable characters: an ape imprisoned in a French zoo; a girl coming of age on a remote horse ranch; sea captains; grave robbers; sisters mourning what is lost, mountain climbers contemplating dusk; populating a landscape of influences modern and ancient. These poems transcend State-imposed borders, while warning that the losses tending to overwhelm us are moral and spiritual as well as environmental: "Our lives are tied together in this earth." With this luminous feast of language, one feels our lives may be tied together in poetry, as well.
—Sheryl Clough
Write Wing Publishing
Editor/Publisher: *Through A Distant Lens: Travel Poems* (2014)
Author: *Ring of Fire, Sea of Stone* (2013)

The natural world not only evokes Alexander's internal habitat, but is integral to it. All things are in constant change, she notes, in "Monochrome" during a seaside holiday with two others: "We are three, writing the day's obituary" and their own. Even in "Hospice, The Villa Marie," a very personal poem about her mother, Alexander considers the "cicadas waking / from their seventeen- years' sleep" when the chaplain spoke of immortality; on seeing a family of deer, thinks, her mother will "have to take them on faith," as she also will "who cannot stand last things." A lifetime passes, she notes "In the time it takes to slice a seckel pear…" and that is exactly how the reader will feel on coming to this collection's final poem-- unable to believe it happened so quickly-- and yearning to go back and start reading from the beginning again.
—Linda Lerner, author of *Yes, the Ducks Were Real* (NYQ Books)

Praise for *Bridal Veil Falls*

Hearts foreclose. Derelict roofs come tumbling down. Near death moments and moments of calamity befall us, yet somehow we narrowly escape. And there are moments when we hang limp as a garden gate, suffering disrepair. In *Bridal Veil Falls*, Carol Alexander offers us all these moments and more. In poem after poem she reminds us we are all in the same fix called life together —whether in precarious alliance or terribly alone, 'so close to another country…all but lost.' One could walk all night, sleepless, or heed Alexander's dictum to "Live, you sore fools, live!" So we must, with the kind of rueful rejoicing and aplomb only a taleteller of Alexander's superb skill can summon to the telling.

—George Wallace, Editor at *Poetrybay* and *Great Weather for Media*

Habitat Lost

Carol Alexander

洞月亮

CAVE MOON PRESS

YAKIMA 中 WASHINGTON

ISBN: 978-0692870105

Habitat Lost

Acknowledgments

Anniversary, *Red River Review*, 2014

Attribution: Blue Lady (1957?), *Tic Toc* anthology, 2014

Awakening, *Eunoia Review* 2016

Between Two Worlds, *The Avocet,* 2016

Balance, *The New Verse News,* 2014

Bridal Veil Falls, *Boyne Berries* (UK); reprinted in chapbook *Bridal Veil Falls,*
    Flutter Press, 2013

Vanishing Species, *South Florida Poetry Journal,* 2016

Children's Stories, *The Journal of American Poetry,* 2017

Dean Street, *Poetrybay,* 2014

Departure, *Bluestem* 2014

Extremis, *The New Verse News,* 2015

Habitat Lost, *Split Rock Review,* 2015

John White, Departing Roanoke, *Illya's Honey,* 2012

Long, Long Tail, *Caesura Poetry and Art Magazine* 2015

Long Time Gone, *San Pedro River Review,* 2013

Piazza San Marco, 1980, *Through A Distant Lens*, Write Wing Publishing, 2014

Port Arthur Girl, *NPR, The Common,* 2012

Shrike Hunting, *South Florida Poetry Journal,* 2017

Skeleton Crew, *Big River Review,* 2013

The Fort, *Boston Literary Magazine,* 2014

The Leaving, *Driftwood Press,* 2016

The Pier at Midnight, *Illya's Honey,* 2014

The Potter, *Poetry Quarterly,* 2012

The Sad Giants, *Big River Review,* 2013

The Time It Takes, *Epiphany magazine*, 2013, reprinted in THEMA, 2014

The Warrant, *Zymbol,* 2013

Rose Lake, *OVS Magazine*, 2011, reprinted in chapbook *Bridal Veil Falls,*
    Flutter Press, 2013

Table of Contents

Starting with *A*

And we would eat only what started with *A*—
the puritanical apple, the mild almond
with taint of cyanide, drupe birthing pale seed.
We tasted avocado, shedding the rough skin
to finger its flesh, bared in summer heat
on glaring days, almost Mediterranean
under the bee-stricken pergola, almost fatal
and the sky juddering under a yellow biplane
like a child's toy, the plane descending
to shear the horizon neatly in two: *shazam*.
In our mouths was Adam's *A*, indefinite thing.
Summer's palate soothed acedie,
for which there is no cure but mundane prayer,
taking the world bit by bit on the tongue
transmuting all forms of its energy-- the light,
the sugar, the bitter, the distaff gathering
lily-languished asparagus, grains of amaranth,
unlovable leaves of the artichoke, ripe green all.

Extremis

Your voice in Saint-Germain-de-Prés is pastis
in a glass of fog, held by an invisible hand.
How phrase this in a nomenclature vivid
as a lipstick smeared at the bar?

In the hotel lobby, Arab girls and boys
praise a wine never to be served
and potted palms are sleeping, curled and dry.

That great beast, the wind, noses pavements
soaked in blood that dries before the world's eyes.

Raised on every bridge are unwavering lights
where once smoked oil lamps strung on narrow streets.

My camera pinches off lanterns and loaves,
a pink dress hung in the galleries
while your meeting, not to be postponed,
is soup and cigarettes under martial law.

Dogs off-leash bare teeth and wheel
at the unfamiliar smells of men.
Muted leaves that missed their moment
when September made an oven of the streets
mostly now have fallen into loam.

I've a little forgotten disaster in these months;
it could be the sound of wind through husks
or a tremulous breath breaking in mid-song.

The Waters of Paris

Stones of Montmartre, glancing saints of Saint Etienne

seen through a haze of nausea: I'd swallowed water from the tap

and a little fever that kept faith all the meters of our stroll

overwhelms even the poulet et frites, a pastiche of straw

and golden skin ordered by the German, the American:

it is almost our last meal, in the sense of an association

propped up by a tarragon sprig--strangely like a Yuletide tree

in bonsai scale, and for the sake of your sweet company, I'd eat.

A lack of something in your eyes, the drifting on white sheets

later in the night, while the thirst for poisonous water

gives me dreams of longing, longing burnt to ash

before the dawn. An embroidered skirt you'd chosen,

purchased as a souvenir, hung limply from a chair;

in the turning of a hip, you stage managed your sleep

long past the ringing of church bells, two coffees on a tray.

Is your fever gone, erection of the morning put to use;

there is an atmosphere of pretense, so that the tickets

marked for our return are more substantial

than the stones of those Montmartre streets

or the staunch basilica of Saint-Denis, repository of kings

and those who antedate the greatest of our noble ones.

You say you've had enough of crypts.

Instead, we take the metro to Vincennes where,

gazing at a circumspect old ape, we grip the cold bars,

learning from its gestures a pure language of grief.

Departure

A path limps to the paddock

where chestnuts and bays

bloom like Michigan maple.

Remember the funny line about goats,

Ou trouvé les petites chèvres méchants?

They're here, worrying geldings and mares

with nudges of their stiff, whorled horns.

Thirteen has drawn first blood,

which brings a girl near to the mares,

swell of their rumps and patient eyes

that look upon saddles with indifference,

champing at the wind-rocked crabs,

kicking idly at blue tail flies.

By a harvester, boots thrum in the dirt,

and a man with a rider's width of thigh

surrenders one glance: not enough time

and there never will be, cartons stored

in the moving van, a map of a city

circled in ink, a name on an eastern street.

This man won't see her bud and swell,

braids take on the sheen of hide,

nor find her trembling against a stall,

pinned to a shaft of light.

She won't know the foals of spring

or the breaking of a brindle colt

or curses stung of a sprain,

reprise of opal frostbite on the trail,

nor again rein in for the sake of deer

breaking the ice shield of the creek:

to be denied at the very verge

where plodded grasses flatten out

and smuts whip the blades to gall,

a corn field falling sick, working

farm run down, all the dudes

gone back to town, keeping warm.

The nag nuzzles her palm,

sidles slyly, bows, walks on.

Skirting thickets of box elder trees,

males and females grasping the wind,

drooping flowers dried and brown—

things draw in. A slip of a girl

may be parceled anywhere,

from creek and field and barn,

from a low scrim of rusty vanes

run amok in November gale.

On the trail, death is everywhere:

garter snake and headless wren,

a tree stricken in the late storm.

By this swale, her hands first froze.

He warmed them with cold,

and her girl's eyes dazzled

at the gold of his hair, muddy boots

by the range, sills caked with snow.

The harvester idles; the engine dies.

Unsaddle here and hang up tack

as a late sun mows day down;

the hour has come to turn east,

to try on early sorrow, unbutton

shadows where the yellow gorse blows.

A Glass of Water

There are one-celled empires in this glass

and in the sweating jadeite pears

rife with tiny colonies.

Spores of fungi rich as bracken,

ferny tendrils branching at the lip: in a single kiss,

our tongues are archipelagoes.

Animalcules in droplets, children of the rain

give nothing audible but churn and flail

in our rivers, wash against embankments,

feed and spawn upon those interstitial tides.

When we drink we become rivers, traveling

through jungles and stony places where the lions died.

Let's wade while the shallow, festering swale

yields some minute life—pond striders mouthing larvae,

sun begetting stubborn forms, the dark shore cabining.

Skeleton Crew

Last bags packed and stowed

gravel echoing no more,

wild rose shunted to earth

by the livid storm—

no sound louder

than the whining of a dog,

no form beyond impress of flitting guests

whose odors linger on unmade beds:

let's clamber down to the pond.

Water has gone monochrome.

Absolution of heat, hairpin clutch of damselflies

mating on the wing, scintillating;

by the drear swag of pines

one rower smoothly cuts the gray

until he rounds the bend, shipping out at day's last.

Pray for him, though the waters are not deep.

Flesh once succulent, bog of things unseen,

tempt him to cruel weeds where he sticks fast.

Anatomy

In darkness we steal bodies in plain grave clothes.
Freshly dead, eyes membranous, modest;
it seems almost a crime to snatch a pauper's rest.

By candlelight we explore their crevices--
four-chambered heart, leguminous kidney, muddy entrails.
We will learn all they've eaten, posthumously.

We whisper, cajole; they stare back furiously,
knowing they've been tricked.

Are silage for our greening field.

We thought only of the kiss of life.

One draws with the silken feather of a goose
coils of dank viscera
while another lifts a lung, imagines a sigh.

Purple-black blossoms on the anterior skin—
this love of everlasting, this anoxia.
All you beauties.

Within, the roil of internecine gases and salt,
a great ship splitting at the hull. A quick draft of stale beer
before we leave them lonely in the dawn.

Ramble: Tree

We mark a tree by its rings, but what remarks the tree?

Maybe the lovers and drifters who have lain in its shade

or the force of winds that snap twigs and scatter dried pods,

and here I think of a catalpa on the corner of Germantown

I passed when homeward bound from school, the winged seeds

enchanted like keys to the forest where a child dwells,

not only the child whose home is full of books and bread and light

but one who enters a wood with hidden beasts and knives,

and not the beasts with the slender toes of lemurs but brutes

who slash and howl, revealed in dreams with eyes that quell,

daring them to shine with any light of their own.

The tree cannot measure any of this, nor the weight of a lynched man,

the bones that rest beneath its limbs, the tough bark seeming to resist,

with roots so deep, earth shudders at its core when axes maim it,

the sap that runs then freezes with the old antipodal sunderings as the world with terrible patience remakes itself by breaking in two;

and this is something the ground knows well, from the ice of the north

to the rutted potholes of the underworld, to the chasm of China

where we dug with ironwood, nothing, nothing, so home to bed

and in the morning the ground was once again firm, and we were not lost

because the tree, like a great sundial, took the measure of every thing.

Bridal Veil Falls

The great Falls froze, and perhaps that is why,
the delights of seeing Hell freeze over,
they packed the honeymoon bags, gassed up the car
and spread the map over their knees, where it caught
the crumbs of the winged repast and the flurries
that tumbled from the sliver of sky.

But then, the thaw, the turning of the wheel.
Water thundered, and great clouds of mist
obscured ridges and roads, slipped up wheels,
dripped from the crevasses and hummocks,
silvering over perils of the last resort
and no guardrails where the road curved north.

It could have been the shortest marriage in the world—
car wheels hanging crazily over the ravine,
themselves splayed across the seat, still breathless:
and the roar of the falls, below the ice bridge.

Sentient, spared, they clutched hands,
then the man sprang out into the untouched snow;
they fled the Chevy for the skein of rutted road.
Stumbling in city heels, the snug hem of skirt
damnable, the woman floundered, white-nosed.

Something was decided on that icy march.
Something, some black ice, the marriage seal.

Fires were banked in the redwood lodge;
their wet coats dried by the sulphurous blaze.
She looked to the man; he looked at the snow.
Night closed in with the claws of a bear.
So close to another country, each was all but lost.

Who was the English girl whose letters you kept?
(And why did I know of the English girl--
words trickle through the crevices and pool.)

The blood on the skirt, the grimace in the eye:
what is that but this body of love,
the ceaseless wonder of things done, and undone?
One wrote a name on the frosted pane.
Beyond, the locked waters waited.

Steamers founder on the Great Lakes, engines burn amok.
There's risk in it and ruin, the freefall into darkness.
It took you fifty years to frame this cautionary tale,
before you scrapped it, handed over the keys,
and we drove away, north to cold comfort.

Rose Lake

In the midst of winter

when the wooden gate, suffering disrepair,

hung slovenly from its post

and a bleak wind blew through the house

with its lone gable, like an afterthought,

a folly or a remnant, a failure of vision,

deserting, derelict of duty, we fled into the marsh

and made something festive of the muck and chill.

Those nesting boxes on their flimsy posts—

a reminder of the isolation, the singularity

of that sweet pursuit of endless repetition

multiplying species upon species—

stood out from the sunken marsh,

the only trace of human endeavor.

You let me hold the binoculars.

Herons stalked among the sedge

and patience was rewarded

by a glimpse of frowsty head and beak.

Massasauga snake glided in the reek,

its tiny elliptical pupil winking like

an allegory we ignored, deliberately,

until we saw the gravid female,

drinking the last rays of refracted light,

its skin giving nothing off

of self-absorbed darkness.

Was there a snake?

Yes.

Was there a garden?

Define your terms.

There was, in fact,

she of the woozy, riven heart,

vs. she of the cold hearth.

There was, like an afterthought,

a child grown surfeited

on the cloying fumes of gasoline,

curled in the front seat,

awaiting the verdict

under a white menace of sky.

When she begged you to bring the snake

back to the marsh you did it,

turning the car east and traveling over

thirty miles of December road

with little light to steer by,

rutted roads passing horse barns

and fields where nothing much grew,

miles past the town limits

and the dim glow of scattered bungalows

and all-night package stores.

We skidded twice in the first gusts of rain,

rain that sent wheels into ditches rapidly glazed

as the temperature dropped in panic.

Twice we missed the turnoff to Rose Lake,

where we'd found those beauties,

but where would you find a sign at night

on such a willful, wandering road?

Round and round you went

on that crazy ride, then stopped for your drink

while I counted the stars and stopped my ears

against the slamming of doors and the throaty laughter

of men arming themselves against the night.

You were drinking to something or in farewell to something.

. . .

And then we came back to it, to Rose Lake,

and freed the venomous thing into the marsh,

then stood for eons in that purifying cold

knowing there was not and could not be a sign.

A miserable crossroads of a night, yet,

conceivably, there was some wisdom in it, after all.

Children's Stories

I. Nursery

The children lie down for a nap, doing anything but.
The one with bright baubles in her hair twists and squirms;
she is already suffering for beauty's sake.

The children hiss *don't touch me, you're touching me.*
Their teacher arranges paper and paint,
a cartoon of the deep, what flits and feeds within.
Though they all thrill to octopus and shark,
few have toed the ocean sand, or carved its isinglass.

The afternoon's game is touch without being seen,
while the victims forfeit some essential dignity.
The braided, bedecked girl can be thought to win
because continual discomfort keeps her sharp as a knife.

When she sees a hand reach for her knee
she slaps at the flesh and bone with a practiced stroke.
No traitorous sleep clouds her thick-lashed, sickle eyes
busy tracing a brittle star.

How she'll translate that waking dream to paint
is the story she must shape, again and again.

II. Knowledge

When my mother asks the butcher to take a look
he sees the red of the bee-stung flesh.
Believing in the efficacy of any man's judgment,
she is quiet while the butcher raises a knife.

He says, *it will have to come off*.
The stinger? *No, the arm.* To be six
is to be credulous, with a smattering of fact.

Which is, in this case, that people do lose limbs.

A butcher shop is not an operating room—next fact.
The pimpled breasts of chicken, fat of baby lamb
don't reassure; only see what a trusting nature can do.
For further information, see the smirk at my dismay.

III. Mother Country

Young Abraham, dragging the goat
to a stone, the haft of volition is in your hand.

Crevasses of wind sing madly
of wonder, of the three blessed days.

Rose-ringed parrots in the wild plum trees—
a flash of emerald teasing the eye.

Motionless and numb in American sneakers
and baggy jeans as the frantic doe screams:
fear like a shaft nearly cleaves your spine.
A knife is passed from hand to hand
but the village has seen you turn aside and fail.

With a belly of rice and meat, a sweet
in pocket to be savored in the persimmon night,
dazed by this strangely swelling heat

cousins with dark, enormous eyes
and bare feet splashed by carmine guts
stare as a man with his expert arm
guides the knife home to the sticking point.
Her delicate legs buckle; the sun falls.

Love Auditions

By the empty tequila bottle, floats a swan. Soft the hiss of monogamy.

In a harsh clime, kindness is like mist; more durable virtues hewed the land.
Once a man auditioned for love and, fearing the nay, stepped through
a handy window to watch a second swan jut from the sedge.

Mind makes covenant with its body, or perhaps the other way around.
Drinkers slip their bonds and look for the swans. Though near, closer still
is the man who so feared love that the window and the dark seemed kind.
Trees around the shore are pale with blight, but the man is a ghost.

Party noises slither from house to lake. The last man to drown here slept in
his boat while the storm guided him down and down. There will be no death
tonight but for small fish swallowed lovingly by the greedy herons,
and dissolution of cloud. Face underwater and face on the shore construct
each other, and the weeds bind.

Hospice, The Villa Marie
for my mother

Shade of the locust tree on the last good day—

ignore hum of a vacuum scourging dust. Sisters shadow the walk

while bees idle by blue hollyhocks, by Mary with her rosary.

We woke today in hope, to find your spoon untouched in the water glass

with its cloudy scum. A dying body, says the nurse, is not a hungry body.

Still, there is this urge to feed, the patient industry of the bee.

Here were once rich farms, and somewhere still are horses

heavy-eyed and blue, their great hearts resting, riders thrown.

What's left to do, but fumble with your oxygen, put to rights your chair?

It's promised you will have no pain, that the fertile locust tree

will outlast many a late-summer day, that we will have our time.

I've never known your truce with the life to come.

The chaplain spoke of immortality of soul, not of its tough, fibrous core.

Yet, there is the endless mantra of cicadas waking

from their seventeen-years' sleep, and a swallow creasing air.

Evening comes to sigh for you, its gossip riffling through the trees.

Breaths drawn out, day pulls in, a sea wall with its mumbled undertow.

My eye parses a family of deer at dusk. You'll have to take them on faith

the same way I, who cannot stand last things, remember birth

while the morphine steals you to the shades, and the doctor says, watch.

Awakening

To reinvent sleep--but the gates have been put up
and where are we now, within or without

in the enormous room of shadow puppets
or the casual ward where they beg for wine,
a suit of warmer clothes; stitch them, they're bleeding.
My mother too-- she is poorer than she looks.

Is the child still in the crib, is this disruption his staccato breath,
must the lungs struggle, dependent always on alchemy?

Beside dripping trees, I marry you. Again and again.
And by the August sea, the glassy shore pulsates with kelp,
and the ocean swallows its artifacts.

I try once more to sleep
(you will say I have slept like the dead for hours)

but the mind is not a self-cleansing organ;
its detritus is vast, measureless.
Let's bury each other up to the neck in sand.

Now we're at a carnival, our parents wearing masks.
Iron strikes iron, the carnies are warming up.

The boy is nearly grown, his broken crib put out for the trash.
And the girl boasts, see, I am swollen, great with child.
But you are only being born, I say.

The far field sprouts striped tents, camels, elephants,
shrunken heads on strings, garish plastic beads—
every tattooed vendor is primed for some exchange.
I think it is time to divest, and will purchase nothing new.

A gathering of family from another, foreclosed life,
sage murmuring of voices, which are inaudible in the day—
English, Yiddish, Esperanto. They came by boat
and slowly parted from black wools.

We take their arms. We become their canes.
Forget we've shoveled dirt over those mouths, those eyes.

But you, lying prone, are welded to my living bones.
You've put aside your bronze spear, vulnerable in the dark.

Are you stirring, love? Because day
cannot stake its tent, or our ghosts burrow in,
if the ritual of waking is undone.

The Pier at Midnight

There go piratical gulls swooping over the masts
and low waves slapping the hulls of docked ships.
The knife of lightning, the lull before the boom,
send us from the spit to the empty boathouse

where the thin attendant, smoking his spliff,
has left the doors unlocked because the storm
assures the dock of its perfect loneliness:

but for two fools creeping in tandem with the tide
that makes so little mark on the jetty hugging shore,
and doused with the spray of quartered sea
stagger abreast in a sudden gale that whips us all

where lobster boats, where ships of rescue capsize,
where the wandering lighthouse beam picks out
the tiny figures tossing in the cold, black waves

and soaked to the very skin around our bones,
we wait with the smoking boathouse man
to hear those marine signals spelling yes, spelling no.

The Iceman

A man went up and down the floes, on the far coast
where archipelagoes of melting ice wrinkle out to sea,
and fuddled nests of ptarmigan and snowy owl give way
to long, deep footprints of the great beast of prey.

So man, charting vestigial ice, takes its doleful measure,
each frail slippage into the waves an icy taste of doom
for the tundra hunters in extremis of recorded time,
for blued eggs of stalky piper and martyred eider duck.

He must be patient as the tundra veiled in ice,
gripping earth through the months of gales,
for company just the cold, impartial eye
that does not blink at the vastness of the task.

John White, Departing Roanoke

When we wouldn't take him on to Croatoan, he wept for the small girl,

a three-years' child whom he might never see again but spectral

in the flotsam of the storm that murdered men. We had lost ourselves

so many that his tale of ghostly souls departing through the trees,

daubed perhaps with garish paints or hunted to the beach,

was nothing more than moaning of the sea or whining of the wind.

Our captain stuffed our ears with curses, dark eye on the tides.

His useless case of paints, his brooding on the filthy shoals

where our ship might run aground, his endless sob of memory

made of him an outcast but for one: I crept beside his fitful bunk

and begged for stories of the brief and barren colony, the red man

shoring up uneasy peace, the rusty Carolinian grouse feeding

in the drying shrub amid the cloud of midges darkening the sky.

I would at that time and forevermore have jumped ship swiftly,

swum the muddy tide to Roanoke and lived among its ghosts.

And on and on the lost man spoke, brushing back his whitened hair,

of New World birds and blessed shores, of black-haired women

weaving shells into their deerskin skirts, pottage of the sassafras leaves

and the ruddy sun like piss of men with kidney stone, like war wounds

hacked and hewed with the flashing knife, the deathly sharpened stone.

In his sleep he muttered freely of the fool who failed in any wise but one,

all but driven with his dreams from his wild, weary Paradise.

I think at last he sat among his maps and copper Indian girls,

whatever he had failed to sell, time withering once-agile hand

until no longer clothed in hopes, he took his stick and paced streets

palled in that peculiar English gray until some vision of the Carolinas

led him on to Ireland, and among its rich primordial green he fashioned

an enduring dream of women clothed in the mist rising off of Roanoke.

Orphans

Three sisters meet on a clinic bench.
Parted at birth, they know each other instantly
by their pointed fingernails
and begin to talk at once in different tongues.

What they say is, you don't know what pain is, fool.

They have beautiful hair, ladders and ladders of hair.

But no, they meet at a crowded quay,
and each licks a lemon ice, flavor of the day.
In untranslatable babel they boast
you haven't tasted ice as I taste ice, you're numb.

They begin to compare their orgasms.
You know how that kind of talk goes.

A man steps out of his boat.
He could give them anything of this world,
emeralds and marrons glacés.

But they flap away like ravens, like crows.

They rendezvous at the city zoo.
Each has her favorite animal but none will admit
it's the wild boar, murderous and uncaged.

They begin to compare their fathers,
men tusked, without a forwarding address.

When at last they meet
it's at the mother's grave.

You don't know what her love was,
the orphans start to weep.

They are thinking again of pleasure,
of the body's secret places—

what they deliriously gave,
what was stripped from them.

The Potter

Imps, we pinched off thumbs of clay; you didn't see, hunched over the wheel,
the devilish heat of the kiln sweating you, matting the unlikely red hair
you'd brought with you from Spain. Bullish shoulders, thickened arms apt
for slamming down the clay, wedging the air bubbles from its flawed mass,
seeking some perfection in this one way:
we called you the Minotaur, shuddering gleefully in the maze of pink dust
 coating the cat, begriming the floors, filtering into our tiny lungs,
your small unwanted visitors tempting the red beast.

The pots were fit for a beast man, mythic in heft and size—big enough,
you liked to say, to stuff a smallish child in and catapult to sea.
The ample threat of it clattered our teeth and knocked our bony knees,
and the pink cat, pointlessly washing its dyed paws, leaped out of your way.

At noon, you let the wheel repine, lowering broken back to the grainy floor,
lifting sandbags with your legs, grunting at the execution of this pain.
We brought the cold beer and the white cheese, food for the Minotaur.

At dusk, you sluiced the must of clay from arms and neck and,
stripped to the waist, the truss binding your mottled flesh bared,
made those noisy ablutions at the trough with grunts and bitter moans.
Each gleaming pot cost you: the ochre, the basalt, the green chrome glaze,
each birthed from great beery belches and curses in the mother tongue.
You casually slammed your wife into the wall so that we came to know
the clay-toned bruises that glazed her arms, slip-gray shadows under eyes.

Cat and children shivered, the woman cursed you up and down,
but all in your orbit seemed bound to you, as you to the grinding wheel.
From your living clay were smashed and spun those blind assassins,
those terracotta soldiers for your cenotaph, slightly crazed but sound.

Port Arthur Girl

Down around Port Arthur the tumbleweed, that mobile diaspore,

flings its seeds in a race with time, dying in a pool of rain or oil.

And what they have is a lot of sky and oil tanks coddling crude

and girls in much more underwear than they wear way up North.

Mining land is deeply scarred and raw, the gravel pits alien,

like lunar landscapes or the bank where Charon plies his trade.

The young ones necking in their cars, the ugly bars, showed you

the rocking road away from that stripped coastal town.

Somehow you made it, broke and battered, to the pounding stage.

We heard you wailing, every labored breath a paean to the act

of love; girls of thirteen squirming in their jeans, electrified,

right there with you banging some bluesy guy with everything

you got and more—ah, pour it out, Janis, tumbling diaspore.

Flag down that glory train and belt it out with whiskey breath

and the stash of speed that lovers said you didn't need.

What can you do if there is simply more of you than the girdled town

and the gridded streets allow? They didn't claim you then or now

in that spectral year when every other page regaled us with the tales

of players dying in their vomit pools, snatching from us just

that small bit more, goading us to play your albums louder so

the bass reverbed and shook the angry neighbor's floor.

Play on, beauty, ravaged, strands of rough hair in your mouth,

the hot ecstatic winds of Monterey resounding like a dirge,

rafting us across that river, to some bright, abiding shore.

Stretching Exercises

My tendons, they sulk like Achilles

as I stroll out under the blush of dawn,

which the old, blind bard with his rosy tropes

saw by the glow of his inward eye, and plant my heel

on a rowan tree, lady of the mountain

whose Latinate name, *Rosaceae*, binds her to Homer

who would have adored the dactylic clouds,

the strophe enforced by the mountain ridge.

In the cramp of my toes testing the soil, the arch

and dancer's bones inflamed because,

past my first age, I'm drifting toward land,

this too would Homer have sung, the long Greek line

catching up to the tale, his men at their oars,

his wayward gods, gods innumerate as grains of sand

at Pylos, where the nimble divinity shed her skin,

as an eagle flew above, perhaps, a rowan tree.

All things are cognate, by their nature twinned, twined:

madness of journeys, saneness of trees, stretching

beyond the bend where mortal eye would see.

Found in a Chinese Writing Desk, or, The Scholars

During the early Song Dynasty, images of the private retreat proliferated
among a new class of scholar-officials.

From a desk lined in red

sprung with a thin brass key

and pungent with oils

of cinnamon and clove,

 of blood spicing the sands

the retiring scholars shake out silks,

roused from years of musty sleep.

In a fragile dynasty,

Yang of Chianglo wipes his pen

on a leaf in a grove by a spring,

his study of Kwei-shan

a hedge against monotony.

Broken shells of pigeon eggs,

tumbled nests in the gorse—

to this paradise, his steps return.

Yu-t'ing-shi works with the light,

palette drabbed from pink to gray

because the sun has left for court,

because the moon's an acolyte.

The moon becomes a lute,

the lute curls up, a pangolin.

Second son, Tzu-yu, he of filial piety,

his cloth spun from mulberry leaves

in the time of the blossoms

shelters at Hsu, drinks cold soup,

poses for the young Yu-t'ing-shih.

The bowl holds the zodiac

with pink crab and lusty ram;

the scholar stirs his broth

and in this elemental stew,

the pangolin begins to play.

43

The word desires to be a thing.

But better wield the pen all day

than fish with a greedy cormorant

or scratch the lice of border wars.

Midge clouds in the loosestrife,

the mating calls of the fox—

the order of the world is here, and here.

Contemplative men, by Yu-t'ing-shih.

Paint mist over the mountains,

webs that snarl the ailanthus trees.

Let the damp breath release,

like water weeping from the eaves.

The Sad Giants

Every child recalls a long-lost flight,

perhaps in humming gardens where black flies

pierce the skin between the bony shoulder blades

and clouds of summer pollens soaked with rain

become a bed of pricking thistle and errant dandelion.

Of tiny gashes riven in the flesh, of nausea so mild

unmoving mercury in reprobate and pouting mouth,

sad giants with their dull, incurious limbs decline

to hear a tale of antigravity, to know a grainy thistle cloud.

But there is memory of such unlikely flight that cannot be

assumed by any child past the age of five, now tethered

by cold smiles and imputations of a nest of silly lies,

then set to drive the willies from the mind, set to work

digging up dry thistles, rooted to the soil with aching shoes.

The children, making caverns of the ghostly laundry lines,

conspire in the telling of quick flight, blood on blood exchange

smeared on dirty fingers pricked by weeds, slashing vows

to honor in some brigand's salty tongue small fantastical tales,

to keep them from sad giants shrinking in this dusty tropic wind.

Habitat Lost

Hawk hectors, craving flesh of our small dog.
In its brush with a sparse beech tree, it flies off-kilter
adrift from the watershed, land of staunch firs.
Bird, hankering, cannot eat stones or the seeds
flung down for more equable squirrel or wren.
Dog's ears flatten, back ridged in a ruff;
something caustic in the red-tail's eye,
but again a wing scathes the tree as hawk recalibrates
the sweet summer air among provisional green,
having half-forgotten flight, gliding like a bat
or a listing kite among the alley of leaves.
Daft in its hunger, daring more and more,
the bird, I think, senses a depth of awe
mortal-made: we too have wandered far
to quell a hunger, haven't yet encountered
passage so vexed as has this aching bird of prey.

For Ghislaine

By the board, pupils like black holes, a North Philadelphia schoolgirl, three years in fifth grade, is fragged by the laughter of the back row. The word is Chesapeake, as in the bay. Cheapskate, she tries, bringing down fire.

Desks etched with curses and pleas, oaken stupor of midday, waxy boxes of cool milk, but she gives off the heat of moving targets, stumbling in the crosshairs. Rungs of chairs implacable, first frost muffles light beneath the blackout shade. We are in the Cold War and could lose even this weak light.

Ghislaine, I wonder at the ignorance: mother plaiting your dark hair, sending you into the tangle of the day, struggles with small hostages. The courage of it, the march to the front lines, the bloodied heels in boots.

My daughter rises now at six, laptop crammed with lesson plans.
She greets children off the short bus, who hardly speak, who twirl, who flap, who cool their heels in the special room. Work well,
I say, for Ghislaine, who must be sixty-three, a grandmother in a street of houses, peaceful now, this winter day.

Shrike Hunting

—after Robert Lowell

A gold fly hangs impaled on a thorn, work of a wintering shrike.
In its provocative way, the butcherbird has struck and passed,
wings pinioned by the wind, drumming out cricket and frog.
It shadows the Commons' stricken pond, whiskered in black ice.
A skitter of sparrows, a scratch and lurch of velvet voles—
once a warden aimed his musket high past carriage horses
while candles burned on hemlocks, and blasted shrikes from the sky.
To the north a stern chill pins the forest to cloud; appetite dulls.
Neither poet nor prophet parse with wire these lame extremities,
nor pack the heart with substance already stiff and dead.

The Trip to the Seaside

Unschooled in death, the children are crabbed.

The grandmother has long been in love with Matisse,

with his split-leaf philodendron and goldfish bowl.

Her tongue tries out the widow word,

resisting its singular thud.

The children have been promised the sea

and although they loved their grandfather,

he has boarded a train on an alternate line.

It's the first of many betrayals,

the drawn shades, unseasonable calamity.

The heat is a slap in a claustral room

that belongs already to oblivion.

A row of shoes waits at the door, toes curled

like yellow leaves. The children learn lack

from the lame, trapped breeze,

from talk permitted in a house of grief.

Thursday they planted saplings

in coffee scoops, just to please the grandfather.

Of all things vegetal he was sapient, a demigod

of sun and rain. Snails are tracing his plot,

the garden having inexplicably grown small.

But we're going anyway, the brother says.

Already he tastes the tang of salt plum,

bitter foam of the waves. He refuses

a slice of cake, the hand mussing his hair.

Where he loved, he now rebels

like the confederate uncle harrying

dust from his bachelor room.

The ingrown house delays them no more—

their timing is ruthless, and perfect.

Stalky and fierce as a gull,

brother wills himself above the talk,

the photos in their shabby deco frames.

Strange that he hadn't seen poverty

in the stoop of brocaded chairs.

By the sea he will breathe drunken air,

pile stones where the land erodes.

The Time It Takes

In the time it takes to slice a seckel pear, removing first its russet blush
perhaps to mash the tender flesh or poach the halves with rotgut gin,
the sky can make a crazy spin, paintings judder on the peeling wall
and the telephone, defying Friday courtesies and plans of sullen kits,

melt in the hand of the distracted cook, who jerks the pan from flame
singeing a strand of dampened hair; the spaniel bitch must be strolled
and in the time it takes to nose the sweet, the sour of the curb
the lungs fill up with water and the sympathetic blister forms a lake.

The infant takes its sugar water from a thumb, sucking doubtful bliss,
the laundry load begins its final spin, and water boils for runner beans.
Or so these common, homely things might happen in some alternate space
where hospitals are wards for someone else, where breath comes easily

and other children, many years now grown, try uselessly to soothe a breast
rising in some desperate dance with air, unconscious of those fairy tales
they've told themselves and all they love these lovely, verdant years—
and that is all the time it takes for the pear to drop, tipsy, to the ground.

And This Was the River

And this was the river, you say. This trickle, this terse complaint, won't water a rat; think hippos at their wallow, slow subsidence of snouts under muddle of gray, and you'll know how far we've come overland, dreaming the coolness of water. We threw away a mound of gold dust richer than our tribe. It choked us besides. Where water sloughed away, leaving corrugated waves like sand spits rife with pill bugs and mites at the low tide, travelers pitched tents and roasted corn and cod. Recall the press of heel and small toe, the streaming kites, the lone black lab nosing the berm. War advances to the saline shores, rusted men with muskets stake out land, cursing the tents. We heard this story years ago, filling our pails at the dripping pump, washing our clothes in the cackling stream: the last fight will be for water. We'll be walking a long time, and the heavy bones of hippos, the fragile bones of cormorants, roll and roll like tumbleweed, and there is so much dust to swallow. This was the river, no place for a woman with child to drown.

The Fort

We liked war games, even then.

The trench by the oak smelled sweet

before the soil was fouled by runoff from the factory.

We tasted dirt and it was black like ripened figs.

We rubbed it on our brows and it was cool

like the solid sky in reckless rills of blue.

We handpicked our atrocities; being the girl,

mine were the worst. Boy's jackets carried me

to the mouth of the fort, and I was invalided out of the game.

Oh, no fair. There isn't much a corpse can do

but lick the earth from between a finger and a thumb.

One of the boys was whipped, usually of a Friday night.

His military father, a teak and khaki ghost,

did his rounds and soldiered on with his belt.

We wanted to kill him, but something else took care of that.

I learned the error of spite, the cold correction of the grave.

55

I longed to stand sentry, to commandeer the fort:

far better than lying in the improvised morgue.

Until the summer rains began, locusts buzzed and sawed.

The knocking of a woodpecker at the gate, salivary rune of slugs,

keloid scars on the legs of the boy, first love, betrayer,

marked all the pause for pity I could take, waiting for another life.

Long, Long Tail

The child caresses her book:
Birds and Mammals of Africa.
Damp finger on a white chicken's tail:
long, long tail. We're learning, late, talk—
not the art of conversation, but words.
Beautiful Echo, ringlets to her knees,
eyes like the pool where lovely drowned,
bare toes at the edge, today: watchful,
hawkish, tongue nearly bitten through.
Good is anything new.
A high scream, a crash in the street;
two cars maybe run out of road.
Sunrise, green park, shovel out betimes
laboring, shifting sand, but for today?
Damp finger on a white chicken's tail.
Long, long, tail.

Monochrome

Wading into the sea

      erases years of industry—

each grain of sand, detritus of a vast machinery,

      push-pull of currents smashing shells.

Forlorn creatures dashed upon land

      gape at the last of light;

she says the sea tells us earth is round

      and he says there's meaning in it all

but we don't take him up on it--no pose

      but gulls magnetized by the little life

spitting into the grayed beach, the wind so chill

      flaying us raw, taunting, turning.

Where the inlet threads to sluggish pools

      crouch fisher girls with rubber boots,

but we feel this fleeting holiday so free, so free.

      Up and down the shore some complex work

is rushing toward undoing: a rip current.

We are three, writing the day's obituary

for the big house lost to taxes, the hands lost at sea;

photographing the vanishing point,

we know we will see nothing but this monochrome.

It's all a trick of the light, a cheat

despite an insidious potency of three, the weird

suffered by every beating thing.

One of us must always walk ahead. And cannot say

mother father where, shovel to pail:

they too loved this ceaseless gluttony of the sea

and licked salt from their lips,

feeding us with a bottomless want, flesh of their flesh—

they've left as we'll leave our own

and the reckless waves fling mussels and crabs

and the stinging flies we call fact and regret.

We imagine nothingness. The one who is best at this

perforce must speak most lovingly.

59

Sweetness

Nothing sweeter for a child

than springtime with the old man—

Sundays free of the shawl,

shapeless in outworn clothes,

lilac pollen dusting the seams.

This taut patch of earth,

tins of seedlings tamped,

is a lesson in economy.

All is husbanded, stalks

and other serviceable things:

the coffee grounds' ripe silt,

dead bees on a compost heap

in kitchen waste and nitrogen.

Fat radishes gleam, and a rose.

Checkers, grief when I can't lose

a red king to him, a fallen pawn.

Hewn from rock, how learn

the foolish humors of a child?

His hands with mineral veins

appoint, bless the board,

gray in the twilight's shade.

I see his iron chair sprout rust,

earthworms part the blades.

Here and There

What she's purchased here and there—

brass weather vane, fish knives

tailed with mother of pearl—are in the guard's dream

as the guard's in mine; he leads us through the Mondrian rooms

of caged light, their jab at flux.

It feels like a maze, flicking her drug-dried tongue.

Saints, having drunk from a humbling cup,

we go round and round those rooms

wanting in, out, of this imposed simplicity.

She shows yellowed dominoes to the guard,

a game he played in San Cristóbal, friends,

though he will not come to her rooms

nor she to the station of the C train.

In a cage, a strand of her ravaged hair,

a square of rose drabbed down with gray.

Things hungered for—*Still Life with Ginger Pot*,

vane, those knives of mother of pearl—

none disguised its provenance

like the distance between here and there.

In Trastevere

In Trastevere, a deep fatigue takes hold of me

as I walk with my child, no longer a child, by a sandstone arch

which curves in Middle Eastern prayer; a happy orphan

on the Tiber's lull, the quarter is an hypnotic state

despite the press of tourists in its narrow alleyways.

All roads don't lead, but circle it--lapping its oils, their scent,

letting the wheels of potters spin, the shimmed, ubiquitous strays slink,

children under the yellow awnings keeping a ball in play.

Left, right, women buying strings of beads, waiters

slapping at flies in outdoor bars, having trudged to the polls

before the heat of the sun, before peeled plum tomatoes

and clink of clam shells make something hopeful of the day.

Two streams of thought: the righteous with their pointed spears

against the nomads braceleted and slim, while the waist-stripped man

plastering a wall, wasps crawling on the craquelure,

wears on a chain an enamel of deep red, both bold and feminine.

Beh, everyone's a Communist, this heard from the dentist

who leans from an antique window for a breath of air,

which on this day in Trastevere is a wisp contained in amber;

I blame my strange malaise on this. And the young woman

whom I bore, herself with a grace and a shining fall of hair,

wears the smile of one who knows that only the old are old.

Between Two Worlds

This boundary between two worlds:

an oil plume glimpsed from the shallows of a bay

as a diving bird cuts water and air—

anemone probing with myriad tentacles,

the violet skate unfolding like a paper fan.

Simple and obscure as under and above

yet precise as the layerings of time

are coral kingdoms, scintillant catacombs,

coeval with rays of bony fin.

Along the spiny coast, faint heel prints.

Just below, frantic mouths.

Day calculates its losses, phyla passing on

into nothingness.

Nature, that radical priestess,

demands her tribute of terrible hymns.

Our creaturely losses, underworld seeds in mouth,

are fast mounting up into rocky cairns—

whole worlds consumed by mid-afternoon.

In the tale of seven brothers we read while young,

only one can hold within himself the thrashing sea.

Dean Street

By the bus stop, dayshift workers gray-skinned in the April chill,
stand lean marbles, granites, samples carved with exemplary names.

She'll have eaten dinner, girded with a bib, in the last fastidious shafts of
light. Our talk was of the flowering crabapple tree,
its quivering, avenging burst of bloom.

Rain blurs into bluestone snow the heft of ancient dolerite. And the fire-tipped
shadows of dusk curtaining the windows of the hall have frightened her.

The bus, its exhalations choked with grime, is bearing down. Even now,
I can't describe for her the weight of this unwieldy, this inhuman thing.

Attribution: Blue Lady (1957?)

Their paintings are the sum of all we know

of the seven ages of man—some slides were lost,

inevitably, and then, we stayed no length of time

to mark bone growth on doorframes,

but like the seeds of the wild plum straggled,

blown off course, to fall where we would.

From the wreck off the coast, this washed ashore,

scumbled on a white field, head cropped off

as if by the whimsy of a fey small child

coloring gamely from the bottom of the page

(amazed that there is no place left to go).

Its subject gazes out with aqueous eyes,

a perpetual prisoner of the wormy frame.

For years, I thought my father painted her

when really, I should have known.

This canvas has the strangest pull,

as if prestidigitation charmed the oils:

thin lady, logy prophetess, her long blues

trailing on yet another six decades,

sipped a draught of wormwood and gall

in beauty like netsuke worn from daily ecstasies,

unmade beds and passing children's squalls,

the lashings from sea-brewed storms,

streams of water seeping underneath the sills.

Father in his post-stroke days grasped crayons,

drawing mermaids on the paper mats while

Mother's lady lingered in a darkened room.

She's made the ocean-blue of nereides

undulating in the eddies of neap tides.

When they had gone, I dreamed we met

in waters off the eastern shoals.

Suite for Dry Gardens

Gracias sage thrives without rain, like wildfire
that fans red blooms into a wake of smuts.
Cheatgrass flays the juniper cones.

A papery char on the herb borders,
bold manzanita hedging the woods.
The piano exhales its resinous breath,
lid circled by a glass's damp heel.

Agency men deploy their scouts; Jerusalem crickets hide.
Confess by the fence how you've mislaid your head
on alien grass, a soiled mattress tucked into dusk.
Only promise not to nourish the errant seeds,
leave the black bears to fatten elsewhere.
Yet, wind will spread the superflux.

A friend kicks low notes from the coastal road.
Like yours, her house teeters on the fault.
Like yours, its rippled glass is filigreed dark gold.
Leona drags her gypsy skirt, hemmed by August fire.

Above the monk's ashes, a chant; Sun himself is abashed.
Maps of self-immolations, Lhasa to Bayan—the sky chokes.
Those who say nothing, hear nothing, tremble
with the mounain, mud and sticks, spin the singing bowl.
Teach me the right way to walk around the holy ground.
If some part of everything, are we this, too?

My phoenix rises, bins the garbage by the back door.
Spent the cold day swathed in wool until the knell
for clear or storm. No starlight in the airshaft.
To the east, oil cans rain death. Bodies torch, a frail fall.

I know what you plant before you dream it;
you've invited me in, and my frowsy thread.
Purple Tapien Verbena. Oat grass. Breath of Heaven.
When the digging is all done, you serenade the cackling hens.
On the round table, you've set all that I adore—
pistachios *au naturel*, a slice of pie, sugar cubes for tea.

Object, Stone

On this May morning, gardening, but not flowers,
having taken an axe to the trellis before dawn
with conviction that the rose is instead a parasite,
not the sign and seal of love, which in any case
has been vexed to the point beyond care—

today it will be the stone that thrust out of snow
all winter long—polar, recondite, grooved on closer look
with striations made perhaps by prehistoric snails.
Stone has mocked the symmetry of the green
with tidy borders of pachysandra and hedge,
recreating every lawn in any town, somehow become
the template by which the deed to be done, is done.

How deep the base of the stone, who knows?
Those who came before left it quite alone or rued
a contest with the brute thing, their failures drab
as a dream with the grays and browns of déjà vu,
so that this gardener in May is truly on his own.

Both he and the stone will have to forgive
before one breaks and the other falls, its granitic core
so dense that the new shovel splits at the haft.
Tasered, his muscles burn with a crippling fire;

tempted by the breadth and reach of his thought
to fossick through the soil, he is thwarted again,
as in the depths of love he found his pleasures stemmed
by the woman who stands with her coffee cup and frown,
whose by your leave he hadn't asked before the trellis downed,
who seems to be an other in this business with the stone.

Lockdown Drill

You'll grow in the dark cubbies, like amaryllis bulbs.

Don't say *death*.

Recall the secretive plant

we settled in the art closet to help it to re-flower.

We've found a metaphor

to nurse into bright bloom, while fire wardens

roam the hallways, going room to room,

each revealing crannies shelved with dry paint pots,

spare boots untagged and left to gather dust.

Don't say *death*. I'll tell about the amaryllis, instead.

For thirty nights blood dripped before his door,

who could not see the girl within the flower.

The shaft struck at her breast each day, but she would live

to see a calyx on its stem, and his heart sinking

on its slow despond which, for some, is love.

Our lives are tied together in this earth,

thin roots a-straggle, shunning the winter light;

which child, then, would raise his head to tempt

a too-bright sun, its metal barrel aiming at futurity?

Ah, the bell at last has rung. Once again, be children

as you were: as you, like all things in their season, are.

Anniversary

He won't logic the steam from a cup,

and she won't order the trout well done.

On the Roman road, arches wear away.

Interstitial pipes of terracotta

snake between limestone bricks.

In those days as now

fish leapt quicksilver from the springs.

Dusty travelers stooped to drink,

their shadows telling time.

Nonius Datus ground his teeth at Saldae,

the tunnel somehow gone awry—

two halves disjunct in montane chagrin.

Despondent laborers spat like cats

or crossed their arms, dreaming of warm beds.

Over and over the mountain

they dug at stony soil, blundering on

by moonlight, by harsh sun.

Rains carved gullies of respite.

Quarries of pale stone have curious lacunae.

Between the graves spring tufts of grass,

but he will not mow them at midsummer;

she will not press them under her heel.

Picking Apples

Because he lacks the mythology,

the boy who might not pass first grade

stands beneath the apple tree

with ashen hands drawn into his sleeves.

It's soon in the year to recommend

but the signs aren't good.

I want to lift him to a branch,

but he feeds on eucalyptus leaves.

Take a basket anyway, I say.

His hands stay in his sleeves

while his eyes, unwashed from sleep,

look on me doubtfully.

Neither Eve nor the planter of seeds

convinces him this field holds anything good

for him. Tussocks spiked with dandelions

seem dreamed to trip him up,

and the eagerness of his classmates

fills him with a nameless shame.

And the beauty of those eyes

the scars across his shaven head

make of apple lore a trivial thing.

I want to say, this is your land.

When I cannot fit the basket to his hand,

I, too, am overcome with shame.

Piazza San Marco, 1980

Turn, and the gold-encrusted pigeons fly up at dusk,
fading to gray against the verdigris of manes. Come and
go day boats bearing the tall and blond, dark and svelte,
photographing horses, their labors stilled, chariot vague
       as air.

A girl in the piazza strains to catch the lisping local speech,
the curious eye of a waiter with his disaffected
dancer's stance; like the bronze horses, he'll give nothing
       warm and trembling away.

So the steeds, taking the last of the sun, raise fine heads
to a wind that sweeps the wide square from the Adriatic
Sea; the girl sips, shudders at the grappa's evil bite, for
which she's paid an unknowable sum, a clink of coins,
       a light touch on the palm.

From campo to campo, she's stalked by boys
with guidebook lore; but desire of horses is everywhere to see,
       and the pigeons roosting there.

See the beasts with gilded muzzles seemingly inclined,
a length apart, wondering at the giddiness in the air,
at the barques of traders losing their way, barred by
       darkness from the rank canal.

None can steal this feast of soft Venetian light, though
the horses think to guard forever the basilica, ignorant
of their fate, their final snorts and pawings rendered by
the girl, hatless at night, last seen searching for
       the bridge to her dim hotel.

Balance

You write, *this is not fun.* Two rockets arc above Tel Aviv
and in the streets, sirens and rubble. I forget you for weeks at a time
until you write about a trip to Mount Hebron, bellflowers, mignonette,
the grandchild's bit of tooth, a logy rock agama in the sun.

I hope you're getting a balanced view. There are bodies in red rags,
pensive cups of coffee after dawn, the drawing heat of the day.
Ordinary death proceeds with its modest civilities, prayers in shul.
In Khan Younis, a family shatters like a crystal cup; no prayer
will bind flesh to soul, no cool wind tame the burning of the coast.

Tell how it is for you, a garden with tall weeds, a son in the hills.
On your land, figs are slowly ripening despite the spider mites,
despite the lack of rain, the sirens louder than a mullah's call.
Heat underlies the very ground where traders shook out silk.

You hope the dusty rocks and rags will be reported truthfully.
You hope, worried by tomato rot, to grow old

Long Time Gone

Wicked blue of dockland

whalers long time gone

throaty whoop of crane

flail of tail and stippled spine

the jarring shouts of ferrymen

the open mouths of boys

refracted duple thrust of pilings

drawing in as slap of wave

draws down the speculative eye:

blue wants only to flow on

past devil's spit and lollygag

of mud flat reeking in the sun

it wants for nothing

jeweling slabs of stone

limpets figuring the dock

where casks of oil

skeins of rope

grease of oaths

stink of cod

blast of north wind

slump of heart

and small clam foot

winkling sand from shell

lie like gray detritus

by the splintery hull

as beached we hunker

down, sand in the eye

our old captains washed

to graves ashore

and widows walk

at twilight

gold and gray:

night thoughts

of a hunted whale

long time gone.

The Climbers

At mountain's midpoint, with shoddy gear,

through lowbush, tramp and slough

of skis etched in shrub, sky flensed, bled out

thin, the air of love's first season,

endlessly replayed against a fractal terrain.

Less opaque—if not to summer cold,

than to each other, shadows on pitched rock,

and we have some things to eat, no guitar.

The second man, a scout whose cabin

lies some distance from the trail,

holds a pinch of evergreen between forefinger

and practical thumb that strums the air

for possible rain, rattle of rocks on fragile berm.

An older woman making her way down,

a rucksack with a towel, vial of iodine:

her heavy dog, its blond fur flecked with white,

slowly lifts its paws. Where it limps,

a stamp of blood. Inside its soft mouth

day begins to melt, and when they pass,

woman and dog, they leave us everything—

great shoulder of the rock, lift to the peak,

volta of a sudden rain harrying us on.

Young men talk of fatalities, no palliative

for vertigo; we should have made ascent hours ago.

Instead a meal of fruit and cheese will suffice dusk,

arctic snow freeze breath; these boys deprived

of the tail gunner's view, fiery bombs exploding

over cities and fields—burnished medal in a drawer—

but in all the world, no one has truly died.

The montane path of medium difficulty:

tumbled with flint rock and cloud,

the struggle to see beauty with hands and feet

clutching at gold grass, the rump slide,

sideways slipping heart gone begging

for the cradle of a funicular, frail circuitry—

the human system forced to right itself,

air turned sugary. Having eaten of such heights,

the lowland spreads out flat and bland;

in another year, our mouths will seek

a lick of salty sea. But this ragged climb:

what the fierce body requires.

Life Drawing

The life model saunters through the door, tardy, startlingly tall.
While she strips the class immediately recalculates;
has last week's model, a European pear, liquefied, slightly oversweet?
　　　Her flavor lingers in a stack of pictures rosy as Watteaus.

Whether to show the pigment-stained fingers, strong and spatulate,
the new model being also art's acolyte, occupant of a studio next-door,
is a question Cézanne in Aix would never pose,
planting small brushstrokes in a field, laborer who'd grasp
the scimitar of bony arms, and the femurs with their stark architecture.

Charcoals limn the facts—a raised cesarean scar, beggared clavicles.
Our desire redraws a belly and limbs fed on the celestial, adding a bit of flesh,
bleaching the hollows beneath those eyes, transforming the epicene.

But we must render precisely what we see, the whole point of the exercise.
Who's to say what she must be, the worn clogs underneath the screen,
scarf and lace bra depending from a hook?

We squeeze oils from tubes, cobalt, ochre, titanium white. Fingers twitch,
jigging after paper and paint. Skin and bone, eat her up entirely.

Why insist on she, rather than I? Joining subject and object
the thinnest of integuments, mussels clinging to shell.
She is doing carelessly what we fear, exposing the mechanism entire,
even the wild jibber-jabber of the heart which wants above all to *know*.

Silence, stirred by the enormous ceiling fan and lost meow of a cat,
scratch of the scumbler, curses of the one who must begin again.
The soles of the model's feet are dusted with clay, the arches high.
She's coming into focus, this uncomfortable woman,
an Atalanta with a nose ring.

At five o'clock, the winter hours wash bowed windows with ink
and the model passes among easels in a nylon robe, flexing her big feet.

On the canvas, by alchemy, hovers young Madame Cézanne,
golden oval of a planed face with the upper lip slightly turned down.
Thoughts of the refusé and spouse persist, bouquet of unwashed smells,
rumpled bed at noon, which knows as much of hope as tulip and snowdrop.
Shadows of dusk smudge our wavering lines, until boldest hues alone remain.

The Warrant

Away again: this country is not what it was.
The counterfeiter's saffron hands ink our warrants:
My queen, we'll take the lower road tonight.
Livid with disgrace, the tarnished metal of your crown
seems a magnet for six magpies riding on the evil air.

Bind your hair and carve your breasts: in this way
we'll cross the border, epicene and dull.

Are you frightened?
Yes, I am.

The yellow jonquils on the writing desk
the papery hands of the forger inventing us again
the yellow moon that spies the thieves upon the wall
the fugitive fog concealing our carriage in the lane

I watch these things through tumbrel eyes—
last time, last names erased in one dark night.

How is it with you, in this wanton hour?
Here is your grey cloak, the fillet for your thinning hair.

Very frightened?
Yes, I am.

Never mind the lives we've shunted off.
We'll cross the border at the gibbous moon.

Echoes

On a notched hill twist rain-wet roots
with droppings of the lost horses.

Saddle molded to the thighs,
a russet, leathery musk
and I'm again in Michigan

watching the dull shadows ripple out;
they strike an invisible fence
and lope away with a bruised nicker.

Shotgun blast feathers gorse with blood,
the report quivering for an instant:

a phoenix of desire.

I feel where my legs once were
and wake to practice a limp—
a hex against the world's sly harm.

It is fever and flux.
It is a mouth that fills and disgorges
a river of leaden things.

It is heartbreak, wheat stirring in the far fields
and the great graveyards of rust.

There I first froze, the gun pointed my way.
There I slept against a sweet hay bale,
to wake in a pool of bittersweet light.

Never my own country; I foundered in
thick snow. Crows, those grim old warriors,
startled, warred, struck bass notes from the air.

Vanishing Species

Say the Great Auk, crushed by a boot, relations crowding the southern coast
for rafts of fish and krill. To kill: a way of anthropomorphising.
The enemy, a caricature, in the servant's perpetual white and black.
Say silvered handmaids of Time, clumped around the bingo table,
integuments of wool in the June heat the freckled skin, which fades like acid
paper, catching sunlight through plate glass.
Say wolves imported from the hinterlands to roam the woods upstate,
dropping pups in the bracken, fresh from a hasty rout,
labors brief, explicit, wordless: yet expressly female, blood on their coats.
At the sanctuary, prescient eyes on a group of boys remaindered from the streets.
Kinship, kind. They, a rough kith prowling the night.
The moon's arc, and shapely Venus; lamplighters tenderly at their task,
anachronistic, fauns where the alley meets unspooling dark.
Say the bright display of the national debt, numbers rioting—
and the feathers and scales disappearing into mud, never to be
reassembled but in the child's machine-stamped puzzle board.

The Leaving

Doves strum the fir, the pair that overwintered here

to grieve the lost singleton, frost on pointed wings.

A woman may wed, her animal warmth call to a mate;

she may plant clematis relentless in ascent, and lupine stalks,

furnish rooms with sound, unremarkable things.

And yet.

Bereft is to have twelve empty plates,

to scrape ash from the teeth, suffer the burning sun

as the necessary steps of going on, go on.

A dervish of sand sweeps through the screen

leaving nothing clean enough to eat.

No water but the fluid of love, visible in her belly's swell.

Veins map the silk roads home.

Quickening, the unborn stakes her claim,

insistent as any creature fully made.

Two wills, one that nulls my offerings—

the day's mail, whole-meal bread, lavender for a bath.

Instead, a mess of entrails left unread, the drying husks of beans.

Her closed mouth, a sickle moon.

It rises in the east, over the garden wall

and the drains from which I pick white slugs.

What will hold this acreage? the tardy, knife-like shoots,

brambles laced with stippled jewels, straining to the ground?

Salt wind creeps through the seams of the house, through every joist,

a word from the Old French meaning, to lie down.

About the Author

Carol Alexander's poetry appears in anthologies including *Broken Circles* (Cave Moon Press), *Through a Distant Lens* (Write Wing Publishing) and *Proud to Be: Writing by American Warriors, Vol. 1.* She has twice been nominated for a Pushcart Prize. Her work can be found in numerous print and online journals such as *Bluestem, Caesura, Chiron Review, The Common, The New Verse News, Southern Humanities Review,* and *Soundings East.* She is the author of the chapbook BRIDAL VEIL FALLS (Flutter Press). HABITAT LOST is Alexander's first full-length collection of poems.

www.ingramcontent.com/pod-product-compliance
Lightning Source LLC
La Vergne TN
LVHW091226080426
835509LV00009B/1181